S0-BEG-825

Longwood Elementary School
Library Media Center
30W240 Bruce Lane
Naperville, IL 60563

WITHDRAWN

RELIGIONS OF THE WORLD

I Am
Eastern Orthodox

❧ PHILEMON D. SEVASTIADES ❧

The Rosen Publishing Group's
PowerKids Press™
New York

Published in 1996 by The Rosen Publishing Group, Inc.
29 East 21st Street, New York, NY 10010

Copyright © 1996 by The Rosen Publishing Group, Inc.

All rights reserved. No part of this book may be reproduced in any form without permission in writing from the publisher, except by a reviewer.

First Edition

Book design: Erin McKenna and Kim Sonsky

Photo credits: Cover and p. 20 © George Ancona/International Stock; p. 4 © RIA/Gamma Liaison; pp. 7, 8, 11, 12, 16 courtesy of the Sevastiades family; pp. 15, 19 © Hazel Hankin/Impact Visuals.

Sevastiades, Philemon.
    I am Eastern Orthodox / Philemon Sevastiades.
      p.   cm. — (Religions of the world)
    Includes index.
    Summary: Introduces the basics ofthe Eastern Orthodox Church through the eyes of a child of that religion living in Chicago.
    ISBN 0-8239-2377-0
    1. Orthodox Eastern Church—Juvenile literature. [1. Orthodox Eastern Church.] I. Title. II. Series: Religions of the world (Rosen Publishing Group).
BX320.2.S44 1996
281.9—dc20   96-1508
                                                          CIP
                                                           AC

Manufactured in the United States of America

Contents

Eastern Orthodox Christian

My name is Anastasia. I am an Eastern Orthodox Christian. I live in Chicago. There are Orthodox Christians in many different countries. They are all members of the Orthodox Church.

The Orthodox Church has one leader. He is called a **Patriarch** (PAY-tree-ark). He is the head of all the **bishops** (BISH-ups). A bishop is in charge of a group of **priests** (PREESTS). Each church has a priest. My brother Demetrius is the priest in our church.

◀ *There are Eastern Orthodox Christians in many countries all over the world.*

Tradition and the Bible

Tradition (tra-DISH-un) is very important in our religion. My brother says that we follow very old traditions. Our church services and prayers are part of our religion's tradition. The Bible is part of our tradition. We read from the Old Testament and the New Testament. We pay special attention to the gospels. These are four books in the New Testament. They tell us about Jesus Christ and his life on earth.

A priest reads from the book of the four gospels during church services. ▶

Jesus Christ

Jesus Christ is the most important figure in our faith. We believe that he is the Son of God. He is our model, our teacher, and our guide. We believe that his life, his words, his death, and his rising from the dead changed the world. He has given us a special relationship with God. He taught us how to pray to God, his father. Jesus asked God to send us his Holy Spirit. Through Jesus' teachings, the Holy Spirit guides us.

◀ *Jesus is a teacher, role model, and guide for Christians.*

The Trinity

We pray to God as a **Trinity** (TRIN-i-tee). Trinity means three. We believe the Trinity is one God. The Trinity is God the Father, God the Son, and God the Holy Spirit. God the Father is the Creator of all things. God the Son was born a human being, Jesus Christ. God the Holy Spirit is God's energy in the world.

This image of three angels represents the Trinity. ▶

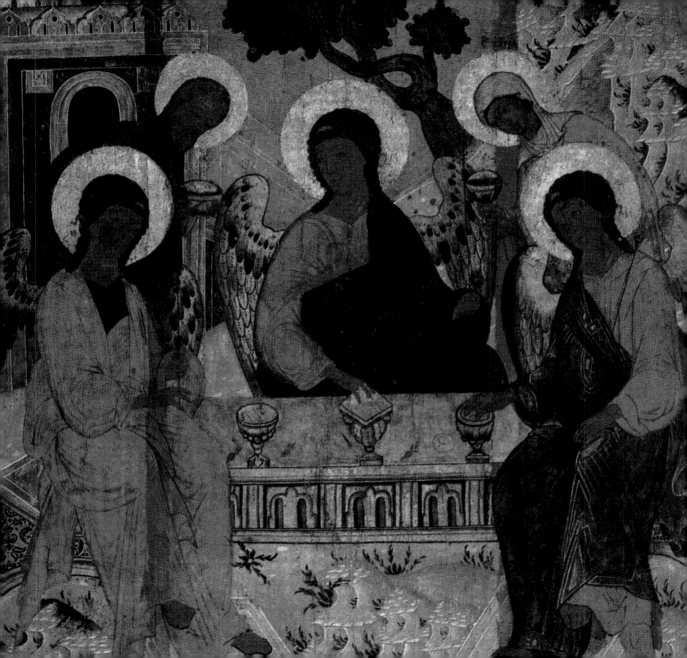

Baptism

An infant becomes part of our religion through baptism. My cousin Irene is going to be baptized soon. She will be dipped in water three times in the name of the Trinity. The priest will put holy oil on her. Then she will receive **communion** (kom-MYOON-yun). This is holy bread and wine. I am going to be godparent to my cousin. As her godparent, I will teach her about our faith as she grows up. I will also give her a cross as a special present.

◀ *A baptism is a happy time for a family.*

The Eucharist

Every Sunday, the members of our church gather together for the **Divine Liturgy** (dee-VYN LIT-er-gee). We hear readings from the Bible. We pray together. Then we celebrate the **Eucharist** (YOU-kar-ist). It is the most sacred event in our church. The priest prays, and the bread and wine for communion become holy. Then my father, my mother, and I receive communion. The priest gives us communion with a special spoon.

The priest leads the Divine Liturgy. ▶

Marriage

In an Orthodox Christian wedding, the bride and groom don't say any vows. Instead, the priest and community pray for them. The bride and groom give each other rings. Then the priest places crowns on their heads. The crowns are connected by a ribbon. They also drink wine from one cup. These things show that they are now joined as one. Then the priest, bride, and groom walk in a circle three times in honor of the Trinity.

◀ *The bride and groom drink wine from the same cup to show that they are one.*

Prayer

Jesus Christ taught us how to pray. Sometimes I pray when I am afraid or need something special, like when my mother was sick. Sometimes I pray to thank God. We pray in the name of the Trinity. We call God "Father" because we believe we are all God's children. My parents say daily prayers at certain hours of the day and night. We also pray together at church.

Prayer is an important part of being an Eastern Orthodox Christian. ▶

Christmas and Easter

The two times of year that I like the most are Christmas and Easter. Christmas is a joyful time. We celebrate the birth of Jesus, the Son of God.

Easter is the happiest time of year. We believe that after Jesus died he rose from the dead and went to God. At Easter, we celebrate Jesus' **resurrection** (rez-ur-EK-shun). My mother and grandmother and I make special cookies and dye Easter eggs red.

◄ *Easter eggs are dyed red to represent Jesus rising from the dead.*

Church and Community

Our church is our **spiritual** (SPEER-i-chu-all) community where we meet with other Orthodox Christians. When I am at church, I feel the love of all my family and friends. I also feel God's love. My brother says that the church is the place where heaven and earth meet in a special way. It is like God's kingdom on earth. I like going to church with my family.

Glossary

bishop (BISH-up) Leader of a group of priests.

communion (kom-MYOON-yun) Receiving and eating the blessed bread that Eastern Orthodox Christians believe is the Body and Blood of Jesus Christ.

Divine Liturgy (dee-VYN LIT-er-gee) Church service at which the Eucharist is celebrated.

Eucharist (YOU-kar-ist) The blessing of bread and wine and taking of communion.

Patriarch (PAY-tree-ark) Leader of the Orthodox Church.

priest (preest) Spiritual leader of a church.

resurrection (rez-ur-EK-shun) Miracle of Jesus Christ coming back after his death.

spiritual (SPEER-i-chu-all) Concerning the soul rather than the body.

tradition (tra-DISH-un) The method of doing things as passed down from generation to generation.

Trinity (TRIN-i-tee) God the Father, God the Son, and God the Holy Spirit.

Index